I0197550

MISSION GUYANA

By

Joan E. Lunney

Published by

Dot Jot Publications

Copyright 2010

All rights reserved, including the right of
reproduction in whole or in part in any form.

Printed by Lulu.com

ISBN 978-0-557-52942-1

Contents

Acknowledgements

Psalm 43:3 "Send forth your light and your truth, let them guide me...."

Psalm 57:3 "He sends from heaven and saves me, rebuking those who hotly pursue me. God sends His love and His faithfulness."

Malachi 3:1 "See, I will send my messenger, who will prepare the way before me."

I truly feel anointed by God to write this book and acknowledge Him first and foremost.

My thanks to June Tuttle, without her, this mission trip never would have happened.

Pastor Germaine and the whole First Congregational Church in Hopkinton, Massachusetts who commissioned us. We felt the Spirit on the whole trip.

The Thimble Pleasures Quilt Guild in Mendon, Mass. supplied us with materials and other embellishments for our quilting projects.

Thanks to Sharon Lippincott and Margie McMaster for reviewing this manuscript and providing comments and suggestions.

Thanks to Petra Matthew, who is an inspiring poet and wrote June and I the following poem:

Joan and June

They came from across the Atlantic Ocean
to this multi-ethnic, multi-religious nation.
Citizens from Massachusetts, a beautiful state in America,
and strangers to this country of many waters, Guyana.

Filled with the Holy Spirit of God
and for sure, covered under the blood,
June and Joan, the names by which they're known,
gave themselves fully and the seeds were sown.

Women of all ages, boys and girls, too
received and were blessed, yes, this is true
With new skills and now a desire to lend
themselves to Him, who His Begotten Son sent.
What a blessing! God is so good, we say
to His people as He opens doors each day,

to allow more people to be members of his family,
and to be holy even as He is holy.

Thank you Joan, thank you, June,
God has blessed you and now you've blessed our hearts.
You gave yourself without counting the cost
to the People of West Demerara in the Guyana District.

Thanks you, Joan, thank you, June,
for you were examples of the living God, most High.
Into homes, schools and shops on the streets you carried
the Love of God, to every anxious heart.
Thank you, Joan, thank you, June.
Continue to labor asking for no reward.
Let the knowledge that you do God's perfect will
Fill your heart always with joy overflowing.
Thank you, we love you dearly,
and sincerely pray that God will strengthen you
to go always where the Spirit leads,
with the good news of salvation, to every dying soul.

Chapter 1:

Introduction

How in the world did I ever get to go to Guyana on a mission trip? The answer to this question goes back quite a while. My first mission trip was to Dominica, in 1996. My friends, Sandy, June and I went as a team to minister to the women and children in that developing nation. We were dubbed "The Golden Girls" by the people on the island. June was an old friend to the Dominicans. She had spent her two week vacations in Dominica as a missionary every year for nine years, but this trip was a first for Sandy and me. Over the span of many years, June made many friends, one of whom was Delsy, the mother of Petra Matthew. Petra married a minister, Telbert Matthew and they had two children, Ritchie and Rachael, who were four and nine at the time.

The Matthew family was assigned to Burpee, Guyana. Guyana is located in the northeast corner of South America, at the point where the Caribbean meets South America along the North Atlantic seacoast.

One day in Dominica, while June was sitting talking to Delsy at what the Dominicans call the old people's pool, she was struck with a conviction that she was supposed to help and support Delsy's daughter, Petra. When June got back home, she wrote to Petra and shared her vision. June started writing regularly, sending financial support as well. This continued for a couple of years. June expressed to Petra that she felt led to go to Guyana and see first hand what Petra's needs were and how she could help meet them. Petra welcomed the opportunity, but was in the process of moving. She said that when they relocated to West Demerara, Guyana, she would welcome the opportunity.

When Petra was settled in her new home, she invited June to come to Guyana as a missionary. June didn't want to go alone, so she asked if she could invite me to tag along, and Petra readily agreed. June and I have one of those relationships where we might not see each other for months, but when we do, we are in sync with each other as if time stood still. On our previous trip to Dominica, we worked very well together and we *knew* this too would also work.

Chapter 2:

Preparation

Many people helped us prepare for the trip. The First Congregational Church (FCCH) of Hopkinton, Massachusetts put a box in their lobby for supplies we requested. When we got to Guyana, our plan was to have June work with the children, and I would work with the women. Petra asked if we could get a word processor so she could do the bulletins for her churches. At that time they were handwriting the bulletins. People at First Congregational Church also gave money for us to buy what we found we needed once we got down there. We converted this to travelers' checks.

Petra also requested a sewing machine. My quilt guild, the Thimble Pleasures of Mendon, Massachusetts, donated fabrics and other sewing supplies. I had a small electric sewing machine that I mailed down to Guyana, rather than carrying it as part of my luggage. One of the women in the Thimble Pleasures Guild worked in a hospital, and told me she was supposed to dispose of several boxes of new syringes, because the size requirements changed and her department was not able to use them. She asked if the hospital in Guyana could use them. Petra was thrilled when I told her about this and gave me the address of the hospital. I mailed them, rather than get in a battle over Customs thinking I was smuggling in drug paraphernalia.

The most important preparation for this trip came during the Tuesday evening prayer service when Pastor Germaine at FCCH gathered everyone present to commission us, and the whole church prayed for our safety, our health, and for God's Will to be done.

It is customary to bring gifts to people when visiting as a missionary. Some people disagree with this philosophy, but others embrace it. The gifts don't have to be expensive or of great monetary value. For my gifts, I went to yard sales. God put nice things in my path, not for me to keep, but for me to share. I strongly feel that I am blessed to be a blessing. I feel blessed when I find 15 gold bangle bracelets for $1; I am blessed when I find a supply of lockets that a crafter is getting rid of and she lets me have them all for a dollar. I am blessed with clothes as well. I am blessed when everywhere I go I find angel pins. All these items went into my stash for gift giving. I am blessed when God gives me a

poem for any occasion and am blessed when June does cal-
ligraphy so well that she can put the words on paper and
we use our combined God given talent for gifts.

While packing for this trip, I included a lot of jewelry. I
also took scripture books, pads of paper, as well as "give
away pens" that I collected, buttons from old clothes, small
toiletry items from hotels, as well as my own stash of fabric,
elastic, thread and other sewing notions. I got pin backs
and other items for craft projects

The suitcase that I carried these gifts in was a large
brown heavy one, with wheels. I'd had it for many years but
it was too large for me to use on a regular basis. I remem-
ber thinking as I was packing that I wish I had two smaller
suitcases instead of this large one.

Chapter 3:

The Trip

Sunday, March 4, 2001

My friend Bea Johnson drove June and me to Logan Airport. When we arrived at 4:30 a.m., check-in at American Airlines was already backed up. June had a backpack and a word processor as carry on luggage. She had gone to a mailing store and asked them to package the word processor so it would meet airline size requirements. They padded it with bubble wrap and covered it with brown wrapping paper, which was taped and tied with string.

The clerk at the counter told her she couldn't take the word processor on board. June was trying to tell her that we did plan for this and had it wrapped to meet the size requirements, but she wouldn't budge. We asked if we could check it — Her answer was "No, you are already at your limit on luggage." The woman then snapped "Do you want to go on this trip or do you want your luggage to go?" The line was backing up, so we just walked toward the gate and stopped on route from the ticket counter to the plane to pray over the word processor.

We asked God for some guidance – if He wanted it in Guyana, He would find a way, and if He wanted it to stay, He would guide us where to place it. Just then someone said "move along." June and I looked to each other with a knowing glance and mouthed "Thank you, God" and we just walked aboard with the word processor. Whew! It wouldn't fit in the outside overhead, but it did fit in the middle over- head.

We made it to Miami and had a delay there. While we were in a res- taurant, we asked a waiter to take our pic- ture. I'm on the left and June is on the right.

Everywhere I go, I look for nice things and this airport was no exception. I found a vendor selling watches. They were beautiful and very inexpensive. I didn't know what I would do with another watch, but I just wanted it. I took my own watch off and proudly wore the new one.

The plane from Miami to Guyana was smaller than the one we took from Boston, but June bravely carried the word processor on board. It wouldn't fit in any overhead there, but the flight attendant got some scissors and opened it. After she took off the paper and the bubble wrap, the bare word processor fit fine. God's Will — we prayed down there. We sat next to a man who now lives in Miami, but still has family in Guyana. He told us the present exchange rate was 160 Guyana dollars to one American dollar.

When we arrived at the airport in Guyana, we were the last ones off the plane. As we descended the steps into the steaming, searing heat, we felt bone tired and frazzled from the day's early start, the challenges we'd faced, and hours sitting on airplanes. Suddenly I felt surrounded by peace as we saw Petra, Pastor Matthews, and Mr. Brown, our driver, standing in the lobby of the airport with huge smiles. They greeted us with warm hugs. The Officer in Charge at the Guyana airport introduced himself to us. I thought he was a Navy Officer since he was dressed in a white uniform. He was genuinely friendly and let our luggage go through without opening it. Obviously God was still at work.

My first impression of Guyana began forming even before we left the airport when I saw children begging for change. A single word, "WOW!" ran through my mind, as we rode in a van from the airport to the Manse. The roads were paved but there were no speed limits. Automobiles shared the road with dogs, cows, goats, and horses — the animals just sauntered along. Our speed was entirely determined by circumstances. It was a unique experience. In spite of our intense excitement, when we arrived at the Manse, we were both so tired we just wanted to go to bed.

The gate needs to be opened manually to enter the grounds for the church and Manse. The church was up next to the road and the Manse was set back off the main road. The entire complex was about an acre and was fenced in. There were two rooms available for us. One was on the ground floor and had an attached bathroom. June took that room. The small room had a plain bed and bureau. and bars on the windows. The padlock on the outside of the door gave me the impression it could be used as a jail cell. The attached bathroom featured a large open soapstone shower with one pipe coming out of the ceiling. The toilet sat on its own platform, elevated about eight inches off the floor on, and looked like it was made of aluminum or steel. Aside from a constant battle with mold and rust, it was impeccably clean.

I took the room upstairs and shared the bathroom with the Matthew family. The bathroom had a toilet with a door, and a separate room with a sink and shower. There was no hot water in the home at all. We were lucky we had cold running water — at times we didn't even have that. The home was built about 20 years ago by the Methodists. It was a two story house, with an integral garage. There was the bedroom that June used, an office for the pastor, and a huge, covered porch-type open air room that could be closed off and locked. Security seemed to be a concern, although we never encountered any danger at all.

The upstairs had a staircase leading into the living/dining room. The living room had a sofa and two chairs as well as a TV, bookcase and desk. There was also another staircase off the kitchen. The kitchen had a propane stove, sink and refrigerator as well as a table and four chairs. There were three bedrooms and one bath upstairs.

In spite of my fatigue, I didn't get much sleep the first night. Dogs barked all night and there were ceremonies going on in the next street with loud music and chanting. I opened the window to let in a breeze since the heat was excruciating. There were no screens on the windows, but I had mosquito netting around my bed. The only furniture in the room was a bed. A small sink hung on the wall behind the bed. I found it interesting that the bed was in the middle of the room, with the mosquito netting attached to the ceiling. There were no pictures or anything on the stark white walls, and the floors were wood. I found the nylon sheets on the bed very hot so I spread my t-shirts beneath me to sleep on and eventually fell asleep.

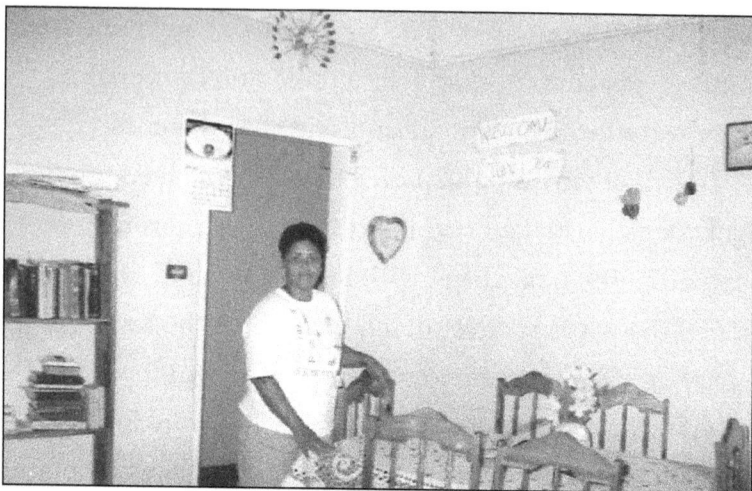

Monday, March 5, 2001

We met Petal. Petra hired Petal to cook for us, clean our rooms and wash and iron our clothes. We didn't expect such wonderful treatment! We also met the Matthew's children, Ritchie and Rachael. The children at first and June, Petra, Pastor Matthews and I ate after the children got off to school. Breakfast for the children was dry boxed cereal. It was customary for them to put water on their cereal. Petal prepared us a rice and bean dish along with coffee and toast. The TV was usually on each morning. We would watch Joyce Meyer's program as we ate our breakfast.

After breakfast we went to the bank to cash some travelers' checks. The first bank we went to couldn't cash them because they were not equipped to do so. We had to find another bank. The next bank was located down a hill from the main street. It had what appeared to be a front porch, and there were guards carrying machine guns. We were told to sit outside on benches until they were ready for us to go inside. There were several other people waiting for service, and the guard called us each in turn. The exchange rate (184/1) was better than we expected.

Outside the bank, Mr. Brown was waiting in his van. As we got to the van, a man approached us with a paper sack. He spoke to Mr. Brown, who in turn told us that the man was an artist and wanted to show us his wood carvings. This was fascinating. We probably never would have had this opportunity at home because we would be suspicious, but we felt Mr. Brown was our guardian angel on this trip and wouldn't let us be duped into anything. The man told us he liked to make sculptures out of wood, and that he sold his work to gift shops. We felt like the grapevine was at work here by having him waiting outside the bank for us. We ended up buying some souvenirs from him and later did see the same type of sculptures in Georgetown when we went to the open market. I bought a carved wood statue of a praying woman, about six inches high for ten American dollars. The way I figured it, he would be able to eat for a week for that and it was a great buy for me to get a reminder of my trip and piece of art work. June also bought several pieces of wood carvings.

After settling our money issue, we proceeded to the local store to get groceries for the people we were to visit that day. We made up four large bags and spent $40 for four visitations. The $10 for food is approximately the equivalent of $80 here in the U.S. The store clerk was lovely. She had a gracious smile for us and told us what she thought the people would need. She said there were not a lot of refrigerators in the area and people cooked fresh foods. Rice and beans were always a good choice. With her help, we also included bluing soap, boxes of cereal, flour, and sugar. She retrieved items from her shelves that were the best buy and what the people needed. We combined the food with other gifts we brought from home, and made up attractive bags for the gifts.

The picture on the next page shows the storekeeper and the shop They have pretty near everything you need, but not a lot of choices of brands. They have open shelves that they keep stocked with the necessities.

Petra, June and I went to the first Methodist congregation and met with the women who would accompany us on
our visitation. The first person we visited there was John.
On the next page is a picture of the way we were led into
his home, which is on the left. He had diabetes and was
blind. He couldn't put any weight on his foot, so he stayed
in bed all day. He was attended to by his granddaughter, a
lovely 18 year old woman. John prays that God will take
him home and away from his suffering. We prayed for
peace and comfort. We also played tapes on the portable
radio, and sang songs to him. I could see the warmth and
love his granddaughter had for him. There was no clock or
watch available at that home so I took the watch I bought at

15

the Miami airport and gave it to the granddaughter so she would know when to give John his medicine. God knows what's needed and provides it.

The homes reminded me of shacks I once saw in the south during the 1960's. The women were dressed very well. They always wore skirts and blouses that were clean and pressed. It also amazed me that they didn't perspire, as I was soaking wet right after I showered.

Our second visit was to Miss William, who was in her mid sixties and Angela, who was in her early twenties. Angela cannot speak, but signs very well. They were happy to see Americans. We sang praise songs and read scriptures to them. They were grateful for the food and the gifts we brought them from the U.S. Each person was very gracious and hospitable. Angela was wearing a shower cap so I asked if she just took a shower. They said "no, that's her hat for company."

The third visit that first day was to Jean and her frail, 90-year-old mother. A family friend carried her out of the bedroom to be with us as we sang our songs and prayed. Going upstairs to their home was quite an experience. This home was built on stilts, about eight feet off the ground. I saw all the rotted boards on the stairs and was amazed that the home was not condemned. The home was a large combined living room/kitchen, with a bedroom off the living room. Both rooms were painted bright blue. Plastic flowers sat on a table that was covered with a plastic sheet. There was no way the mother could ever get downstairs to go anywhere so there she sits. Hopefully our visit gave her some comfort and diversion. She smiled when she saw us.

The last person we visited that day was in the process of building her house so we sat in the open concrete section with her and prayed. Here's a picture of her in the cellar foundation.

Doing visitations was a stretch for me. I thought I was going to just minister to women at the church functions. But the Holy Spirit filled me and I felt a peace I never had before. He not only comforted me, but enabled me to pray out loud in a way I could never do on my own power. I certainly grew in my faith this first day.

Tuesday, March 6, 2001

We got up and had breakfast. I opted for toast and coffee. We read our devotionals and prayed for our day to be filled with His will. We used June's room to do our planning and preparation. In there, we could spread our papers and other materials on her bed and work without being disturbed. Another advantage of using her room as the office was that it could be locked when not in use. I also used June's shower so I wouldn't intrude on the pastor and his family during their morning routine.

On this day, as I ducked flies that were intruders in the room, June said "I have something to tell you before you use the bathroom."

"Oh, OK?"

"When you flush the toilet, frogs jump out."

I burst out laughing, then said "That's cool, they can eat the flies." and we both had a good laugh. The frogs were about an inch long, brown, and they blended with the metallic color of the toilet, so there's no way of telling whether they lived there or came in with the flush. They just hopped around the place and soon were out of site. I braved it and approached the toilet with caution, looking for the little guys. Sure enough, once I flushed, out they came. What a wonderful balance of nature!

Once again, Mr. Brown picked us up. He had a little brown bird about the size of a canary in what appeared to be a homemade bamboo cage. We named the bird Brownie and he rode with us in the van the rest of the time we were in Guyana.

Mr. Brown took us to another section of Guyana, outside Anna Catherina. A large turnout of women and children were gathered there in another church that came under the jurisdiction of Pastor Matthew. He has a total of seven churches in his district.

Because there was only one Pastor, Petra and some other women served as lay preachers in all the churches each Sunday.

Some of the women had accompanied us on visitations the previous day. Some women also met Petra for the first time. Our purpose was to minister to these women and children by sharing our testimonies before we formed small groups so we could do crafts and get to know each other on a more personal level.

June had found the Guyana National Anthem on the internet and printed the words along with graphics so the young children and youth could color and make a wall hanging. I took backs for making pins, the batting, buttons and other embellishments as well as fabric that I bought

preprinted with scripture and pictures. Each woman made
a pin from the fabric by sewing around a preprinted picture, stuffing it with the batting and sewing it together.
Then they sewed the pin backs and embellishments on
them. Some took sets to show others. I had mailed a sewing machine to Petra, but when we tried to use it, it was
jammed up. This was probably due to the heat and humid-
ity. I also forgot to pack a measuring tape, but as things
turned out, hand work was much more rewarding and we
didn't seem to have to measure the fabric, since it was preprinted.

June and I each gave our testimonies. I was never
comfortable speaking in public before this trip, but the look
on these people's faces as I spoke gave me encouragement

and the ability to speak my heart. I spoke candidly of my trials and how God got me through so I could encourage others. A line in a poem I once wrote said it all "Put me in a situation where I can tell of my salvation and let them **know** it came from You."

The women wanted to color the Guyana Anthem. They didn't get much paper in Guyana, and if they did manage to get some, the moisture and heat spoiled it. The classrooms were taught by the blackboard and memorizing method.

The next part of our journey took us out to a site where a work team from the Methodist Church area in Wisconsin was helping to build a new church. These people looked like they were of retirement age. They were sawing boards outdoors and carrying them into the church.

The outside shell appeared to be nearly completed. However, the finishing touches, such as a walkway, were missing. Petra wanted us to see this church and talk to the work team in hopes of our bringing another team down to finish the job. As in many mission projects, one team starts the project and hopefully another team will come in and finish it.

The church was very small, only about 20 feet by 20 feet.

On the way over to this work site, I noticed several elaborate buildings, and was told they were the new mosques. They looked to be five or six times as large as the new Methodist church. I observed that the newness of the mosques, their Byzantine look, freshly painted white and oozing a "wealthier life style" were leading people away from the Christian faith and into the Muslim religion.

When we got back to the Manse later that afternoon, I managed to nap while June gathered the neighborhood children and told them the story of Daniel. She made paper lions and used old puzzle pieces to glue onto the paper for their manes. I went downstairs as they were finishing up. There were 22 children and one adult.

That evening we went to the church in front of the Manse and had a meeting and craft classes with the women

of the church and their friends. I did pins again and June
did calendars and banners.

Wednesday, March 7, 2001

We visited four people and took them gifts as well as food.
Ten American dollars sure buys a lot of food such as rice,
corned beef, flour, baking powder, macaroni and cheese,
black eyed beans, bluing soap, powdered milk, and hand
soap. My observation is that the people eat very well. We
visited a 77-year-old woman who was very spry. Then we
went to the home of a 90-year-old woman who lives alone
and is doing OK with the help of her neighbors.

We also visited a young girl named Horna, who was

born with what looked like warts on her body. She was in her late teens and not able to walk. She lies in bed all day. A team of Canadian doctors somehow found out about her and sent her to Canada for an operation, but it was not successful. Her three-year-old nephew, with her in the picture below, is her caregiver during the day.

The house was built on stilts about 8 feet high. It is customary to remove ones shoes when entering a home. I walked upstairs and took my shoes off at the door. While we were praying over Horna, I felt something on my legs. My feet and calves were full of tiny red ants. I quickly brushed them off my legs and feet trying not to interrupt

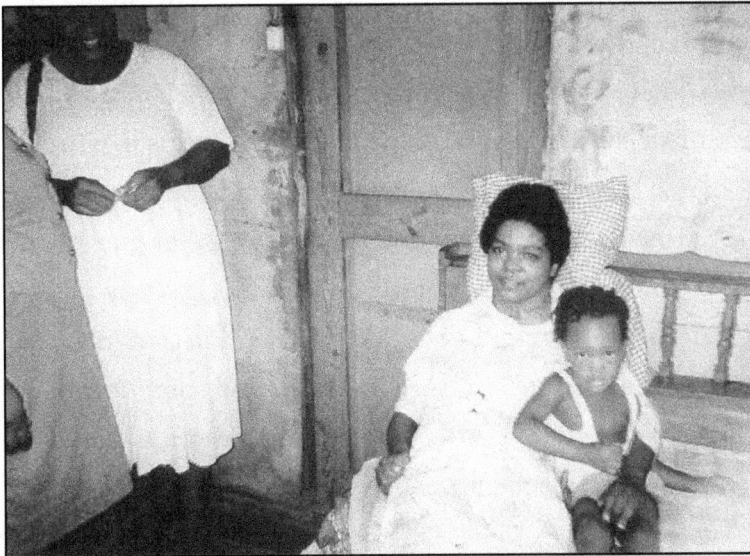

the prayers, but as I glanced at Horna I got a glimpse of her eyes. She seemed to be saying "Why bother? No-one cares anyway." Somehow she touched me more than any other visit. June still sends support down there for her through the woman that brought her to Petra's attention. I felt the need to send down sheets because she didn't have any on her bed. You cannot send sheets to Horna without sending some to her friend who told us of her great need so I mailed them both a set of sheets.

Thursday – March 8, 2001

We were riding in Mr. Brown's van and the radio was on. God gave me a special gift that day. Back at my home in Uxbridge, Massachusetts, my next-door-neighbor, Freddy Velez, had just cut a CD with his group, El Trio De Hoy. He gave me a copy of that CD, and I played it while driving in my car. The song I especially love is "Breathe into my Life". Imagine my astonishment when, on that particular day in March, that song came on the radio, there in Guyana! I found out when I got back to Uxbridge that my neighbor and his group were in Brazil and somehow the Guyana radio station got hold of his music and began playing it. I felt very special that day, hearing that song as a message straight from God telling me we were breathing His love into the lives of the people in Guyana.

We went to Rachael's school. We asked the Deputy Superintendent if we could do an after school program on Wednesday and Thursday

the following week. June would teach the kids, and I would show crafts to the teachers. They said there were many religions at that school, but she would send home a note with each child and ask if they could attend a *Christian After-School Event with the American Women*.

That event was very well attended. Petra and June had more children than they could comfortably handle, but with the help of the teachers they were able to copy many papers and give each child coloring and papers to take home. The teachers all stayed after school so I could show them various sewing projects. I read some poems that I wrote as the Lord guided me to share with them. Nearly all the teachers attended. One of the teachers attended school in New Jersey and was an ordained Minister, but because she had a handicapped child, was working part time as a pastor and part time as a teacher

I was having a problem dealing with the heat, hyperactive kids, and confusion. It was hot, I had a headache, and one little boy kept hitting me in the stomach, thinking was that he was playing with me. I was ready to pack it in and leave right then. This heat was more than I could tolerate and I just wanted to go home. June prayed for me saying that Satan was using people there to make it hard for me to continue. She was right. God did give me patience and understanding and I did overcome that struggle.

That night we went to a Lenten Service, and only four people showed up. One woman in particular expressed her problem with burnout. She was trying to do so many things. June gave a wonderful testimony. I found out more about June on this trip than I did all the years I knew her. She too had personal struggles in her life and through her faith she was able to overcome them. June was able to relate very well to the young woman with burnout.

Petal cooked delicious, well-seasoned meals, and cleaned our clothes every day with no washer or dryer. She washed them by hand in a large tub in the yard, dried them on a clothesline, and also ironed everything. June and I tried to take clothes that we could wear without ironing and leave for the women when we left, but Petra hired Petal to take care of our needs, which she did so with great appreciation from us. Today I had a Coke for the first time in six days. Thanks, God!

Friday, March 9, 2001
We woke up to no running water. Pastor Matthews gave us each a bucket of water that he got from a neighbor, and a large plastic tub. We took a plastic ice cream container and

I went first. Taking half the bucket, I managed to wash my hair and dump the water over my body like a shower. The water was cold, but it felt good.

The water for the home was in a large tank on the premises and was filled by a truck and pumped to the home. The pump broke that day so the Pastor had to get it repaired. Luckily the neighbors helped with this task.

We had seven visitations on this day. In between the visitations, we went to the Senior Center. They were doing a blood pressure clinic. June did a craft class there and I assisted her. I spoke with the Director of the Senior Center and we swapped addresses. I was later able to provide materials for them to use — recognizing a need is one thing, distributing materials is another.

I feel blessed to see the care and concern of the caregivers, usually a daughter or granddaughter or a neighbor cooking and caring for the elderly. We met a pastor, who is a retired missionary and now lives with his daughter and granddaughter.

We met Walter, one of the parishioners at the church in the town. We visited his mother who lives next door to the church and watched her son crochet a shrimp net. I saw kittens and a parrot just hanging out near the home.

Everywhere we go we see cows, bulls, goats, dogs, and some white bird that hangs out with them. Every animal seems to get along with the other animals. Even the various religious faiths of the people of Guyana, the Muslims, Hindus, Christians, get along. It's inspiring to see this in action.

We visited a blind woman and an elderly man. People live well into their nineties and don't look their age. These people were so happy to have our visit and prayers.

Saturday, March 10, 2001

We went to Georgetown shopping for a copy machine and found no Staples or Office Depot here. We arrived at the copier store and were seated in chairs arranged around a desk. A salesperson sat down with us to explain the various products they had available and helped us to make a decision. Our choices were limited to what they could readily get shipped in, but even so, it took all morning to complete this simple order.

We did an outreach program at a church in the suburbs. That church was an outside church with a small one-room shed-like building. The outside was equipped with benches as they have their outdoor services there. A black-

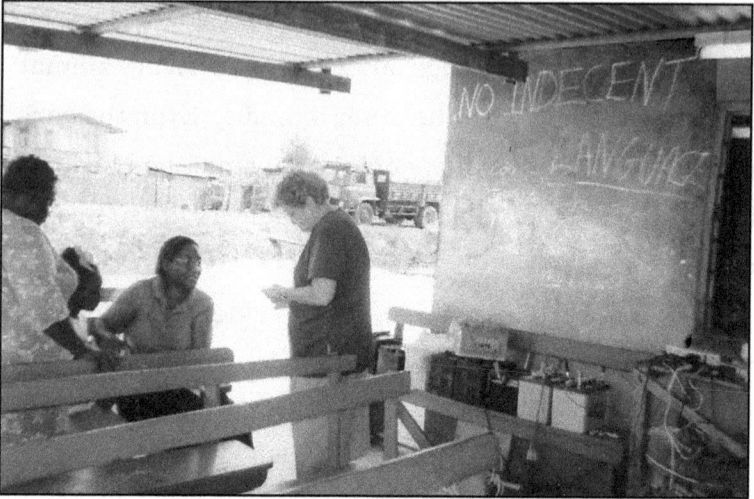

board was attached to the side of the building. On the blackboard was written "No indecent language."

It was a Hindu holiday and some of them wet their bodies and put colored powder all over it – red, blue, purple, pink. Only a few children showed up for our program, but while we were attending to these few, some curious Hindu girls came by. I asked if I could take their pictures, they

readily agreed. Another example of mutual respect of religions – they all get along well together.

Mr. Brown is so patient. He waited

several hours in the heat for us to do our program. I enjoyed working with the kids today. We did a little skit and gave everyone a part. We had printed the words on paper and gave a paper to each child. One little boy in particular stole my heart. He was about 10, and couldn't read. I didn't know whether it was because he didn't know how, or because he couldn't see the words. I coached him along. As the time came to say his words in the skit, he ran off and I asked him where he was going and he said "I need to take a urine." His colorful choice of words was his way of complying with the blackboard.

On our way back to the van, June stopped to show some of the neighborhood children what we were doing at the church. I dubbed June the Pied Piper because she seems to attract children wherever she goes.

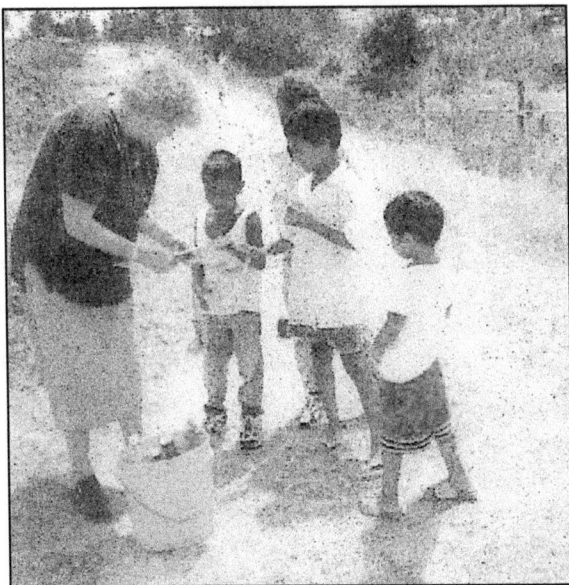

Sunday – March 11, 2001

June and I went to two different churches with Pastor Matthew. He asked us to give our testimonies at each service of how we came to know the Lord. Neither June nor I profess to be public speakers, but we were both Spirit driven and gave our testimonies — no rehearsal or notes, just from the Spirit of God! After services, a couple of people came over to me and said how my testimony inspired them. Thank you, God! The people who attend services all dress as if they were attending a wedding.

In the afternoon, we attended a Sunday School session. The church was in much need of repair. The man who usually cared for the church, a part-time carpenter, electrician, and general handyman, was stricken with a heart attack. No one else pitched in to pick up the slack so the church was needy. Then we took public transport down to Good Fortune, where Petra and Pastor Matthew were having a preachers' meeting with the other regular attendees in the church. The public transport system is like a taxi or van service. The vans and cars have a plate identifying them as public transport and they just ride back and forth. When you need a ride, you just stand there and wave to one going by. You share the ride with whoever else is in the car at the time. June and I shared the ride with several other passengers.

In the evening we went to a church and participated in a Bible Study. To my astonishment, I realized that the dark objects soaring overhead were bats flying around in the church while the music was playing. Nobody seemed to notice the bats. I ducked my head whenever they flew by and was surprised that they didn't bother anyone else. This goes along with the acceptance of all things in Guyana, even bats. We got back to the Manse around 8:30 p.m.

Monday – March 12, 2001

We did seven visitations today. Each one blessed us more than we blessed them. The Holy Spirit continuously engulfed us in joy and peace. We hired Mr. Brown again this week because of the number of packages we had to take. Originally we were only supposed to have the services of Mr. Brown for one week and take public transport the next week, but today we had extra packages.

We met with women at Vergin Newman. Bridget, one of the women in Petra's church, took us to the first visitation; then we met with the other women to continue with the rest of the visitations.

Camile, a parishioner from another church, invited us to her home for a craft session. She owns a store in front of her home. I showed the women how to make the bags to put plastic bags from the market in. June did a session next door with the kids. Camile gave us supper — Indian Style with no utensils. I forget the name of what we ate, but it was good. She even gave us some to take back to the Manse with us.

Tuesday – March 13, 2001

We went to the store to shop for three families and three women from the church met us there. It was pouring rain so we put on plastic ponchos that we brought with us. The women had umbrellas. As we walked down the street in our ponchos, children stopped and laughed at us. It seems they never saw ponchos before or maybe we were the silly ones, the heat from the plastic ponchos was more uncomfortable than the cool wet rain. We were dry and hot, and they were wet and cool. I guess it is pretty funny at that.

George and Joan's home was our first stop today. Although he had had a heart attack, his wife Joan was the actual person we were supposed to visit, but she had a doctor's appointment and wasn't able to meet with us. She has varicose veins and needs an operation. So we prayed over

George and played our tapes. We had left the other packages outside, next to the building near the gate. While the music was playing, I looked out the window and there was a dog sitting next to our packages looking towards the house. He seemed to be enjoying the music and guarding our stuff. He sat there like he was at attention, not moving at all. You had to be there! As we were leaving, George cranked up his radio and was playing his own Christian tape as we walked away. What joy!

This was very meaningful that a man would let women minister to him. Pastor Matthew told us that men do not usually go to church — it is considered a woman thing. There were very few men in churches we attended. Pastor Matthew never heard of Promise Keepers. so therefore none of the men in Guyana had either.

Public transport took us to meet with Agnes and Simon. Simon had a stroke and Agnes takes care of him. Again, we prayed. Simon was a carpenter who used to do things for the church, but now his stroke makes it impossible for him to do carpentry work.

When we were walking back to get the transport, Leonora asked us to stop by the home of a woman named Rachael. She no longer went to church and Leonora thought while we were in the neighborhood, we might encourage her. Time was pressing us and we almost said "no" but something led us in there. After talking to her, June asked her if she wanted to receive Christ in her life and she said yes, she did. I had to see it to believe it!

Then off we went to the neighborhood of Camile, where we were yesterday, to visit Ruby. Ruby has 13 children, and now has her youngest daughter and twins, plus another child, living with her. Ruby has diabetes. She asked us to pray for her son, who is 20 and has a "disobedient spirit." We did. Then one of the women who was with us all day had her son take us back to the Manse in his car. No seat belts, would you believe.

Wednesday, March 14, 2001

We went into the government-run nursery school where I taught the teachers how to make placemats, while June, Petra and Roxanne made noisemakers with the kids.

In the afternoon we went to the new church for a cottage meeting but no one showed up. Petra and Roxanne walked around looking for people while June and I sat on the wall of the new church. A woman from next door came over with the keys. She said there is no cooperation among the congregation. We prayed with her for a spirit of cooperation to engulf the church and the district. Now that the work team left, there is still a lot to be done to finish the church, and cooperation is a must.

Then we took public transport back to the Manse and the four of us had a Bible study at the church in front of the Manse.

Thursday, March 15, 2001

We went to the Preschool again today. I showed the teachers how to make various items with the limited supply of fabric I had left. We managed to make some scrunchies and placemats, as well as potholders and pins. My supplies were dwindling. I also read some inspirational prayers I took off the internet before I left home and some of the poems that God inspired me to write.

In the afternoon we went back to the Leonara, the Government School, and I taught a second group of teachers. Yesterday, they asked me to teach them to make things that they could teach the children to make. So today I had to stretch to find a new idea. I used an idea June had shared last night, and brought in masters of "The Card Master" and the "Guyana Anthem", things that could be copied, colored, and made into wall hangings.. I also showed them how they could make beanbags for the children to play the game of bean bag. They learned quickly. I

had enough time to show them how to make scrunchies –
these were a big hit, since nearly all the teachers have long
hair.

The Headmaster of the Leonara School took the time
to invite us into his office and chat. He told us he was in
New York "thrice" and also in Atlanta, Georgia, and Flori-
da. His friends there couldn't take the time to show him
around because they were too busy. He was glad to get
back to Guyana where the pace was a bit slower. He was
very gracious to us and didn't hesitate to let us do a Bible
Study in the school. He said he would send a note home
with the children to let the parents know that we would be
there so they could decide whether their children could attend or not.

We took public transport back to the Manse.

Friday, March 16, 2001

We held the last workshop of our missionary journey at
Virgen Nieugen today. Only a couple of women showed up.
We saw a woman walking down the street, and June called
to her. The woman was carrying a bag of baked goods she
had made that morning to sell at the market. June asked
the price for all of them, then bought them all and invited
her to stay for a Bible study and crafts. June said "You stay

for our programs this morning since you don't have to work." The woman agreed.

One man showed up, so June took some people and did a skit with the man as "King." I showed the women how to

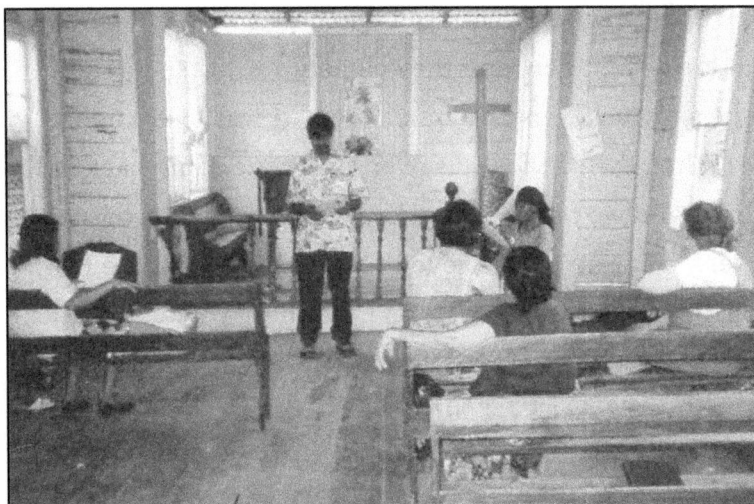

make our craft projects. They were so grateful for this knowledge.

After the skit, June asked if anyone wanted to accept Christ into their lives, and the woman with the food accepted him. She told us she was a Hindu, but accepted Christ anyway.

We had the afternoon off and rested. Petra told us at 4:45 we were having a service at 5:30 at the church out front. When we got there, it was actually a "Goodbye Celebration" for us. Each congregation we visited was represented, and each Congregation gave us a gift. Pastor Matthew gave a nice talk and related our visit to verses of scripture. Each representative told of the impact we had on their congregation. They put two chairs up front for June and me to sit down, and they came up with the gift and some sang us a song. Some danced. It was overwhelming!

When the service was over, everyone came back to the Manse and we had a party. Everyone brought food and cakes. We were so overjoyed. Never have I felt the Holy Spirit in my life as strongly as I did these past two weeks!

Saturday, March 17, 2001

Feeling refreshed after rising early and taking a cold shower, we headed to Georgetown. Pastor Matthew had a 9:00 meeting there. We went along for the ride and went shopping. We went to the market and a jewelry store. While we were there, the proprietor got a call from Jimmy Carter's aide to pick out three pieces of gold for him. We saw a Habitat for Humanity house Jimmy Carter was building nearby. He was also in Guyana as part of the elections team. Elections were to be held the following Monday.

Sunday, March 18, 2001

Two weeks had flown by in a blur, and it was now time to return home. As Petal and Petra helped us pack, Petal admired my brown suitcase that carried all the supplies. She told me she was saving up to get herself one. What an opportunity, once again God just said "give it to her." That made my luggage lighter for the trip home, and she was thrilled to receive it. When I got home, I bought two smaller suitcases on sale, and I still use them today, a much better deal than the huge one I left behind. We also left the balance of our supplies behind so Petra could continue to minister to the women in her church.

However enriching it is to go away, it's always nice to come home. I thank God for giving me the resources to do this Missions Trip. These trips help put the world in perspective for me, and I appreciate more fully what He has given me in my life.

Chapter 4:

Reflections

Since this trip to Guyana, my life has taken on a new direction. I have become aware that Christianity is only one facet of a many religion. I was brought up Roman Catholic because my mother converted to marry my father. Later in my life, I was pulled into a great uplifting and nurturing Congregational Church — First Congregational Church in Hopkinton, Massachusetts. But that is only a small cross-section of religion. No one can honestly say that they understand any religion other than the one they have practiced. In Guyana, people of all faiths are accepted without prejudice, assuming that each is worshipping a common God. But what about the United States of America? Much of the time we seem more preoccupied with legalities than with faith. Can we make room for God in our midst? Can we stop quibbling about "legal" issues and just praise Him for giving us all life? Can we stop quibbling about differences in our faiths and embrace the commonalities? I hope so.

I reflect on the calmness of the people of Guyana and thank God that He gave me this opportunity to see another culture and enjoy the differences and likenesses we all share as part of the human race.

About the Author

Joan Lunney has taken several short-term mission trips, while living in Massachusetts.

She now lives in Monroeville, Pennsylvania. Joan is a quilt artist who has done presentations called "He Lets My Quilts Tell the Story to Give Him the Glory" at various women's groups, as well as talks on the history of quilting.

While president of Quilt Company East, a local quilt guild, she hosted and produced a community television show featuring various quilt artists in the area.

When her term as president ended, she realized that God gave talents to many other artists and now does another community television program called "Start With Art, " where she features various artists in the community.

You can e-mail Joan at lunney444@comcast.net.

www.ingramcontent.com/pod-product-compliance
Lightning Source LLC
Chambersburg PA
CBHW061514040426
42450CB00008B/1621